To
Chris
thanks for caring

Maggie

ANOTHER WAY TO LIVE

How and why it works.

By Maggie Clay, Ph. D.

ISBN 0-9748054-0-8
First Edition
© Copyright 2003 by Margaret L. Clay, Ph.D.
Revised Final Draft - 9/06/03

Published by
Montmorency Press, Inc.
(Montmorency County Tribune)
Atlanta, MI 49709
(800) 929-5324

Table of Contents

Acknowledgments

This is a blanket acknowledgment of the numerous wonderful people who have helped me all during my life to become who I am and to produce this compendium of my thoughts and philosophies. If you've known me or influenced me in any way, you are one of those. Thank you.

For those of you who gain something from reading this book - or from interactions you have had with me in other ways - share your own wisdom and experiences with others who can learn from you. They need our input. Perhaps they will join us in promoting a direction for the social evolution of our species which fosters interdependence and mutual respect - and nudges us toward creating, on purpose, one harmonious and interactive world.

My special thanks to Pat Murray McConnell who conscientiously edited the manuscript for this book, leaving it much easier to read and to understand, and who gave me many valuable insights about how to navigate the world of publishing. To Tom Young, publisher of the Montmorency County Tribune, who converted my manuscript into this book, I am forever grateful. For thirty years I dreamed of putting my accumulated skills and experiences on paper for you to share. These two people actually helped me do it!

Foreword:
The Task At Hand

There are probably no new ideas in this book. Instead, I've combined familiar ideas in new ways to bring new insights about how and why some of the things we're involved in turn out well - and how and why some things don't. We'll examine things you already know but maybe haven't thought about in quite this way before. You'll also find me using "old sayings" to support my concepts. I believe that, if they have lived this long and still describe familiar behaviors and outcomes, we can learn from them.

My object is not to try to tell you how you should live your life, what you should believe, or what choices you should make as you pursue your career. Those are now, and will remain, your responsibility. Instead, I want to share with you some important observations, ideas, and experiences that have enhanced my own life. They help me to live comfortably with and to understand better the world that I see and live in every day as well as the spiritual commitments which bring meaning to my existence.

This is not a scientific tome. That doesn't mean that my observations have no scientific underpinnings. Professor James Grier Miller and his colleagues at the Mental Health Research Institute (MHRI) of the University of Michigan spent twenty-five years developing the general living systems model represented in his book *Living Systems* (published in 1978). His book has spurred further research throughout the world on the common characteristics of living systems - ranging from cells to supranational systems - and the evolutionary dynamics which produced these phenomena.

In the twenty years that I was a principal investigator at MHRI (including my three years as the assistant director), I learned to appreciate the implications of their research for understanding the way human beings survive and prosper in this ever more complex social world in which we live. This book is my attempt to build a bridge between the world which collects all this wonderful scientific knowledge and stores it in academic jargon in scholarly libraries - and the day by day world in which most of us live and function. A lot of folks may benefit from this wisdom if it is offered in plain, everyday language that they can understand. That's what I've tried to do.

The living systems model has provided me with a handy way of linking the varied phenomena that we'll explore. However, my concrete speculations have grown mostly from my own life experiences as I travelled through nearly four-fifths of a really amazing century, the twentieth. It included the great depression of the 1930's, two world wars plus the "undeclared" ones in Korea and Vietnam - topped off by the Cold War with Russia and the first Middle East skirmish with Iraq. Invention of the atomic bomb, flights to the moon and Mars, and the Internet - plus such other notable events as the vote for women and "really" freeing the slaves - also occurred in the twentieth century. The first few years of the twenty-first century suggest that the fireworks certainly are not over. So, perhaps what I learned on my life journey as an eclectic generalist may yet prove useful to someone besides me.

As we travel, I'll tie a lot of the phenomena which we study to the evolutionary processes of our universe which, many scientists tell us, started with one or more big bangs billions of years ago. Out of these explosions grew the stars and the planets. We'll land on the planet which we call "Earth" and briefly observe its non-living systems. Then we'll glimpse how, as Earth's evolution continued, very simple living materials began to organize into the complex world that we live in today. As you begin to picture how the laws of nature work, you should become better equipped to make choices which allow your own ongoing efforts to prosper under those laws. Make no mistake. <u>These laws are still operating.</u>

*   *   *   *   *

Beginning your journey toward "living another way" requires that you learn to "think another way." Start where you are now. It's a big world out there. The trick is to discover what your part of that world looks like and where you fit into it. You must make those discoveries for yourself, though lots of us will try to help. We'll share our own experiences and the wisdoms and biases we have gained as we lived those experiences - sometimes whether you want us to or not. But ultimately, in fact regularly, it is your right and your responsibility to listen to what we have to say, watch the ways in which we either do or don't practice what we preach, and choose whether our wisdoms and biases can be useful to you. Not all of them will be. The trick is to listen carefully, so you don't miss the things you can use, and so you can tell the difference. Then just discard what doesn't help you.

Information can help in a number of ways. It can reinforce what you already know or believe. Or it can help you to look at the familiar in new ways that you haven't thought about before. Sometimes, more rarely, it will acquaint you with a whole new set of facts or ideas. Hopefully, the experiences you have had in your own life have already been helpful in all three ways.

Perhaps I should emphasize that what I'm proposing is just as true for the contents of this book as for other inputs. I have touched on a number of things which I think might be useful to you. Take what you can use and feel free to make it your own. Discard the rest. Some of it you have heard before, and most of it you'll probably hear again. If by then it is more useful, that's the time to absorb it.

7

Remember that "living" is an ongoing evolutionary process of becoming. It's dynamic and keeps changing as you go along. And it always moves forward. That's important because it means you can never go back. Whatever you do and whatever you learn is "from now forward."

It's crucial that we learn from the experiences that we have, so we can remember and continue to use what has helped us along. We also must learn all we can from our mistakes, so that we don't repeat them. We all make mistakes. That's one of the most important ways that we learn. So feeling guilty or ashamed about making mistakes is a waste of important energy - which needs to be used more constructively in learning new, more productive behavior.

Let's explore for a bit what your new place in the world is going to look like. The first question is "where do you want to go?" followed by "how do you get from here to there?" I'll be your guide as you start up this road. It's one that I've traveled for over three quarters of a century! For me it has been, and still is, both exciting and personally fulfilling. Hopefully, that will be your experience, too.

When I was a student, most of us believed that you got your education first. Then you found employment and kept working until you retired or died. And almost everyone expected to get married and raise a family along the way. Since life expectancy was much shorter, lots of folks never got to retirement. In any case, we somehow figured that once you graduated, at whatever level you entered the work world, you had all the knowledge and skills you needed to pursue your chosen field for the rest of your life.

Of course, there was a sort of expectation that we could, by "on the job" experience, work our ways up the ladder to better paying, more responsible jobs. But our fund of knowledge and skills changed so slowly that the concept of continuing education as a necessity to keep up with the field didn't seem relevant to most of us. It had better seem very relevant to you now if you want to move ahead in the world of today.

The other thing that seemed to be true back then was that each of us progressed toward our own career pinnacle separately. Our success depended mostly on our own skills and the extent to which we were self-sufficient. We were, in some very real ways, in competition with everyone else, needing to know more about everything and to be better at whatever we did than our neighbor.

*   *   *   *   *

Perhaps the health field offers a good example of how that worked. The doctor was our God. He, or even then, occasionally she, made all the decisions and got all the credit when things went right, though not necessarily all the blame when things went wrong. Rank has its privileges, including assignment of blame!

Nonetheless, the concept of a health team, where each player makes a unique and important contribution to the success or failure of their joint endeavor, was unfamiliar to most providers of what we then called "medical" services. About the only folks who understood what I was talking about when I asked about interdisciplinary health teams in those days were the public health workers. That is why I, a research psychologist, joined both the Michigan and American Public Health Associations in the late 1960's, even though psychologists and public health workers seldom worked together then. I needed opportunities to exchange ideas with people who believed, as I did, that prevention of disease was at least as important as cure, and that the job would get done better if we shared our diverse skills in attacking the problems which concerned us all, but which none of us appeared to be solving alone.

I have never been sorry, by the way. Even though they didn't have a niche for me, they always made me welcome. And though I think we still have a long way to go in developing imaginative collaborations, psychologists are often regular members of health teams today. Since many of today's most pervasive unsolved health problems have compelling psychological components, it's a good thing that we're finally getting together in earnest.

Like just about everything else, the old medical model of providing health services is changing drastically. I think this has come about as a natural result of the knowledge explosion coupled with a similar explosion in services available - plus an increasing concern of our general population for our own health and well-being. We went through a period when doctors tried to meet these needs by becoming specialists and referring patients to other specialists for problems outside their specialty.

Of course, such specializations continue, but we've discovered that the coordinating glue that held those endeavors together was often missing. When the two hands treating the patient were on different doctors, the left hand often didn't know what the right hand was doing, and the patient seldom had a clear picture of how the treatments fit together to mutually enhance her or his health. That's an important shortcoming when you are trying to treat whole people instead of assorted diseases. You probably have already discovered that we whole people "are much more than just the sum of our parts."

With high technology playing such an important role in modern medical practice, more and more auxiliary staff are required to do all the things that most doctors were not trained to do. Without mutual respect and good communication among all these players, including talking to each other in language they all understand, it becomes much more difficult to provide adequate services to patients. Managed care adds the complication of having to justify and pay for these assorted services provided by assorted people.

But this isn't true just for health care. Organizations of all types are getting larger and more complex. Many projects require teams of people with different amounts and types of skills and experiences to assure successful outcomes. Knowledge about how and when to use those skills and experiences together to solve a problem or to get a job done is crucial in today's work world.

You may be called on more than once to help out colleagues who never really learned how to work with each other to meet common needs. And by the way, the more complex our world becomes, the more our satisfaction with our own achievements will be enhanced by the fellowship we experience as part of a dedicated team, accomplishing together what none of us could accomplish separately.

*   *   *   *   *

Beyond these generalizations, it's hard to be specific. The particular opportunities that come to each of you, and how you choose to respond to them will vary a lot. If the prospect of new ideas and new challenges is exciting to you, the sky is probably the limit. The old saw that there's always more room at the top than in the crowd is still true. Those willing to take the risks of responsibility and run with them are always in demand.

One of the reasons that taking such risks is scary is that, once you get out of school, people generally expect you to do it right the first time. You don't get much chance to practice. I encourage you to make a friend of failure as well as of success. Don't be afraid of either. Use both as opportunities to learn more of what you need to know to do better next time. Even though it may not seem like it when you're in the midst of either a foul-up or a triumph, there will almost certainly be a next time.

A very good way to get some of that practice when you see a new arena that you want to enter is to become a volunteer. During the second world war, potential draftees used to say that only suckers volunteer. That hasn't been my experience as a volunteer, though if I had to volunteer to go somewhere and kill other people or be killed - which is what we were asking those draftees to do - perhaps I would feel differently.

Many of my most rewarding achievements have come as a volunteer. True volunteering, as I have experienced it, means choosing to use your energies and skills to accomplish things which mean a lot to you but which aren't being accomplished in the usual order of things. It's an unfortunate fact of life that people are much more willing to pay you to do the things that they want done than the things you want to do. When the two are not the same, volunteering can provide some of the satisfactions that otherwise you might never experience.

Volunteering can also provide opportunities to develop or enhance your knowledge and skills in areas otherwise inaccessible to you. And it's a way to practice without needing to be perfect from the start. As an added bonus, it often provides a chance to meet and work with new and interesting folks that otherwise you might never know.

But I would caution those of you who are new at this game. Resist the temptation to volunteer skills, time, or services that you can't provide. Once you volunteer, do it. Or if - for whatever reason - you find that you cannot do it, let the organization or person expecting your help know right away. If you volunteer and then don't do it, it won't get done! And the things we volunteer for in human services usually very much need to be done. Often, people will keep hurting until they are done.

Chapter 1

Doin' What Comes Naturally

The story of evolution was born as the cosmos (universe) raced through the Big Bang and began creating and developing <u>non-living systems</u>. These non-living systems came first. They brought with them certain common principles of behavior. Gases formed and produced galaxies full of stars and planets containing assorted chemical elements and strong magnetic forces. Astronomers, physicists, and cosmologists are still discovering and learning about these phenomena, <u>but they've been there all along.</u>

Evolution has been going on for nearly 20 billion years so far, and it is, of course, still proceeding! As soon as combinations of those elements and forces on the planet Earth made it possible to sustain life, evolutionary processes resulted in <u>living systems,</u> eventually including us. Every living system is a collection of nineteen subsystems whose processes create changes over time. In fact, living is process, resulting in continuous change. "Process" can be described as "getting from here to there" and all processes occur in a structure. The structure on which our living systems are trying to survive and prosper is the Earth.

And why should you care about living systems? Because we people are living systems, and the more we know about how those systems behave, the better decisions we can make about our own behavior. In fact, Homo sapiens (our species) is the only living system whose behavior is almost exclusively determined by choice. All lower forms of organism have evolved with most of their patterns of behavior already wired into the entire species. That is, members of the species all behave in about the same way. They have little or no choice.

Humans, on the other hand, are always making choices, and the choices we make largely determine how we live and how well we fare as we proceed through life. Living systems are open, natural systems that require significant inputs, throughputs, and outputs of various sorts of matter/energy and information in order to live. Processing these is what living systems - including us - do.

*   *   *   *   *

Perhaps we should begin our look at living systems by exploring the concept of "community." Nearly all of us spend most of our lives in some sort of community. If we define "community" in its broadest sense as "some number of people having common ties or interests, living in close association, and subject to the same laws and regulations," then most of us live in one or more communities as we pursue our lives and our ambitions. Each of these communities is a true living social system, and we, its members, are also living systems and subsystems of the community.

For instance, we take in food and drink, and our bodies break them down into fuels to restore our energy and materials to repair our injuries and contribute to our growth. That's the inputs and the throughputs part. The outputs are what are left, and they leave our bodies as wastes. They go back into the environment, but in a very different form than before they were ingested. If any of those things don't work right, we're in trouble. If they do, we grow and prosper.

This may sound pretty obvious, but left alone, natural systems, including us, tend to move toward the lowest energy state possible, and natural events proceed toward states of greater disorder. This is called "entropy" and is a function of the second law of thermodynamics. So, unless they want to go downhill and die, living systems - that's us, remember - living systems must become proactive, to see that our inputs not only sustain

14

us as we are but also allow us to grow and prosper. To go uphill against entropy, we must remain open, and have continuous inputs of both matter/energy and information, the matter/energy for our bodies, the information for our minds and spirits.

We living systems produce and break down many substances in the process of sustaining ourselves and growing. So, periodically, we may feel very good, and be very effective, or we may feel lousy, and have times when nothing goes well. To complicate things, both learning and forgetting are also going on all the time. So, just as we need food and water for our bodies regularly, we also need regular opportunities to interact with other people to keep our minds and emotions healthy. Communication is important because walling off living systems to prevent these exchanges across our boundaries will ultimately result in death of the system.

The concept of communication is a lot trickier than it sounds. It isn't just me saying something to you. Communication occurs only when you actually hear what I say and understand it in the same way that I meant it. The fact that the same words sometimes mean very different things to people with different histories can be, and often is, the starting point for misunderstandings among us, particularly when we don't realize that we do not understand each other. So, if we want to get along, listening to each other is at least as important as talking to each other. As someone once pointed out, there's a reason that we have one mouth and two ears! And when you want someone to understand you, it is vital to use language and examples that he or she will comprehend, as well as to speak slowly and clearly.

*   *   *   *   *

To complicate matters even more, we're not the only living systems. The folks who developed General Living Systems Theory defined seven levels of systems: cell, organ, organism, group, organization, society and supranational system. They discovered that all these levels have important characteristics in common. Cells, organs, other organisms as well as us, families and other groups, communities and other organizations, societies, and supranational bodies like the United Nations all obey the same basic rules. They all need to take in things which will help them live and prosper and get rid of forces which move them toward decay, disorganization and destruction. And they all need constant exchanges of materials and information to do this. Isolation is not good for living systems. Remember that. That's why we need each other.

By the way, cells and organs are also subsystems of organisms, and we organisms are subsystems of all those other bodies, the families, groups, communities, organizations, societies and supranational systems. Larger, higher level systems also have <u>emergent capabilities</u>, which enable them to accomplish things that lower level systems can't achieve. However, lower level systems often profit from the accomplishments of the higher level system of which they are a part.

Each of the seven levels (cells, organs, organisms, groups, organizations, societies, and supranational systems) evolved by a process of "shred-out" - as if each strand of a many stranded rope had unraveled progressively into more and more pieces. This involves progressive division of labor, and differentiation or specialization of each subsystem -occurring from the cell to the supranational system.

Every one of the nineteen critical subsystems whose processes create change over time was essential for the continuation of life in its particular living system at every point in this evolution. If any one of these subsystems had failed to carry out its processes, even briefly, the system it was in would have ceased to exist. For that reason, evolution did not eliminate any critical subsystems. Therefore, all nineteen are in each living system on Earth.

The components which carry out the processes of the subsystems are led by the "decider"- the subsystem which controls the entire system - causing the other subsystems and their components to interact. At the organism level, this decider is usually called a "brain."

Living systems may also have symbiotic or parasitic relationships with other living or non-living systems to take the place of useful subsystems they need but lack. They all work together to form actively self-regulating functions with the common purposes and goals needed to keep the system going. And they all exist together on that amazing living system called Earth.

I mention this to impress you with how important it is for us to learn how to live together cooperatively, so we can all contribute to the health and prosperity of those systems of which we are a part. If we want to thrive, they must thrive, at least the ones that most directly affect our lives. That's why it's so important that each of us find our niche and contribute our bit to the systems to which we belong.

Let me give you a really outrageous example. Suppose your heart, which is one of your subsystems, decided that it wanted to be your stomach instead, stopped doing its job of pumping blood, and tried to start digesting food. It would do a lousy job, and you'd be a goner! Instead, what really happens, when you're functioning well, is that both your stomach and your heart know exactly what their jobs are, as well as how they relate to each other and the rest of your organs, and they all work together in perfect synchrony to keep you functioning as a healthy organism.

Another, perhaps more familiar, example occurs in team sports. On a well coached team, each member not only knows

and what that entails, they also need to
‍.o relates to what other members of the
s also true of a good orchestra, by the way.
‍.iow it would sound if each member didn't
‍.t they were to play and when to play it while
‍. composition with a bunch of other musicians,
all ᴜ.   were playing different parts and using different
instrumeṇ. ʔ A good conductor has helped them all learn to play
together before they offer a performance.

*   *   *   *   *

At all levels of organization of living systems, from the
cell to the supranational system, what the system is and does is
a function not only of the components and events within the
system, but also of what comes into it from the outside. The old
saying "we are what we eat" is markedly visible in too many of
our young people whose constant snacking on fast foods adds
pounds which will be more and more difficult to shed as they
grow older. Similarly, a living system alters the environment
around it by what the system introduces into that environment.
Who can doubt, in today's polluted and often over-populated
cities, that our large, exhaust-producing vans and diesel trucks
significantly reduce the quality of the air that city residents
breathe?

Another characteristic of living systems is that they tend
to evolve and become even more complex. A cell is already a
complex system. Cells aggregate and become tissues. Tissues
aggregate and become organs, organs aggregate and become
organ systems, and organ systems aggregate and become
organisms. That's a rather simplified version of what really
happens, but the point I want to make is that every human being
is a collection of cells which have gone through each of these
levels of organization to become a very complicated
collaborative collection of living subsystems, indeed.

Ordinarily we don't think of a person as a community of living subsystems (i.e. the digestive system, the circulatory system, the respiratory system, the urogenital system, and all the various organs that interact to keep us alive and well) gathered together to achieve a common purpose (i.e. survival). But, in fact, that's what we are. However, if we do consider a human being this way, we can begin to understand how important it is for all of these subsystems to be able to send and receive information and cues from each other so they can collaborate to accomplish their common purpose - to keep the person living, acting and reacting, thus allowing the organism's survival needs to be met.

$$* \quad * \quad * \quad * \quad *$$

The major communication network for a human being includes both the nervous and endocrine systems. And the complexity, effectiveness and efficiency of these subsystems in assuring such synchronous functioning is nothing short of miraculous. The illustration becomes even more relevant for our purposes when we move to the next higher level of living systems, the social organism; that is, groups of people, collaborating to achieve common and separate goals. What does a "group nervous system" look like? Most of us haven't given it much thought. As we contemplate social evolution, we'll need to think about it a lot.

I like to use the following illustration because it points up the really superb way that, in each individual organism, necessary supplies and messages get where they need to be in the form they need to be in - at just the right time to allow the organism to survive and prosper. It also allows us to see more vividly how primitive are our mechanisms for achieving the same ends in our communities. Compare how poorly we - as the subsystems and body parts of the social organism called the group - send and receive information and cues from each other in order to meet the needs of that group.

Many, if not most, of the social problems we grapple with in communities are a function of inadequacies or downright failures to get necessary supplies and/or messages where they need to be in a utilizable form at the time they're needed. We either don't receive or we misunderstand each other's signals, often without the sender realizing that they've been lost or misunderstood. We seldom clearly agree about who will do what—or even about who decides what needs to be done.

Can you imagine the confusion in your body if your heart tried to do your liver's job or didn't share your lungs' mission of circulating oxygenated blood throughout your body? Is there anywhere in our communities where we even come close to such successful collaborative enterprise?

Instead, in our communities, our commitment to acquiring and utilizing new information to help us solve our problems or achieve common ends is only beginning to evolve. It's still mostly lip service—partly because we comprehend so poorly how to get such information, much less utilize it in a timely and appropriate fashion once we have it. However, more and more, the use of web sites and e-mail on the Internet is becoming an indispensable tool which allows us to find, utilize and share information with each other more easily.

*   *   *   *   *

I suggested earlier that walling off living systems to prevent exchanges across their boundaries results in death. Entropy will always increase in walled-off living systems. The consequent disorganization will ultimately result in termination of the system, (Use it or lose it!) This is just as true for societies and supranational systems. Every time we close our borders to inputs from other nations which might enhance our own diversity, we encourage entropy. Isolated nations are in real trouble, though it may take some time for this to become obvious.

The recent destruction of the World Trade Center towers in New York City by the al Qaeda terrorists, as well as the concurrent and ever growing conflict between Palestine and Israel, illustrate and highlight what happens when two or more culturally diverse societies fail to acknowledge and respect each others' needs and beliefs as they try to exist and interact with other nations and each other.

Since, like it or not, our world is rapidly developing a largely global economy, it's high time for nations to listen to each other more carefully and to try harder to play " win-win" games in our dealings with each other. In other words, the more the needs of all players are addressed and, whenever possible met, the better off all of us will be in the future.

In living systems, many substances are produced as well as broken down, and both learning and forgetting occur. There are continuous flows through living systems as they maintain their highly organized "steady states." A <u>mutuality</u> exists among the components of a system. Each component contributes to the processes of the whole and receives in return a portion of the benefits derived from those activities. An orchestra of instrumentalists can create musical sounds which, in combination, enrich the presentation of their work in ways that each musician alone could not accomplish.

This mutual interrelationship also extends across levels of systems and subsystems. Cells and organs get nourishment from foods procured by the organism of which they are a part. The employees of a firm do work and are paid from that company's profits. Likewise, member countries of a supranational system (such as the United Nations) get benefits from its communal activities to which each of those nations contribute.

21

Sometimes the benefits are not equally distributed to component systems at lower levels. Such violations are pathological and can lead to the decay and termination of the entire system! The success or failure of major corporations may be importantly influenced over time by the difference in rewards given to high level officials and lower level employees of the firm.

In the recent corporate breakdowns which began with the Enron scandal, the management teams of large corporations engaged in fraudulent schemes which netted them millions of dollars, bankrupting the company and wiping out the savings of most of their employees and shareholders. This is a prime example of the perils of not sharing benefits across all levels of an organizational system. It has had devastating ramifications on the economic health of the United States as well as for other nations participating in the same semi-global economic network.

*   *   *   *   *

We seldom think about how fragile our living systems are; yet they can exist only in a certain environment. Outside of a relatively narrow range which occurs on the surface of the earth, any change in such variables as temperature, air pressure, the availability of water, oxygen content of the atmosphere, or intensity of radiation produces stresses to which living systems cannot adjust. Under such stresses, they will not survive.

At each living system level, while matter/energy and information processes go on with flows from input to output, the governance or control of the system maintains all related variables within steady state ranges by negative feedbacks or "homeostatic balance." These negative feedbacks damp down either increases or decreases in each particular variable to maintain its stability.

Living systems either contain genetic material (DNA), presumably descended from some primordial DNA common to all life (biological templates), or they have a charter as their template - the original blueprint or program of their structure and process from the moment of their "origin" (social templates).

Life is process and continual change - with all processes occurring in structures. Living systems theory provides useful underpinnings for our journey through evolution because it describes concrete systems that actually exist in time and space, and it honors the constraints that go with such existence. Living systems have specific locations in three-dimensional space, and they participate in changes occurring on Earth over time. The model also treats the production of artifacts which are created by living systems, but which, themselves, are non-living systems. Using these concepts, we can deal with the subject matter of both biological and social systems as real concrete systems in three-dimensional space rather than as theoretical abstractions.

All Nature is a continuum, organized into patterns which repeat themselves, theme and variation, at each level of living system. These similarities or differences are proper concerns for both scientists and leaders of organizational systems - such as politicians, educators, philosophers, economists, industrialists, and, certainly, futurists. The more closely we combine scientific findings and organizational processes to allow comparisons across levels - as well as clarification of relationships within levels - the better we will understand the ramifications of our evolutionary dynamics, and the better choices we will make about the way we live.

To order additional copies of Maggie Clay's book

ANOTHER WAY TO LIVE

send this form with your check or money order for $12.95 per copy, plus $2 per order for shipping

Make checks payable to *Northeast Michigan Community Partnership*
and mail to

Northeast Michigan Community Partnership, Inc.

3022 US-23-S Suite C • Alpena MI 49707

(A portion of each sale supports prevention programs of
Northeast Michigan Community Partnership, Inc.)

- -

Please send me _____ copies of **Another Way to Live** @ $12.95
plus $2 per order for shipping. I have enclosed a check or money order for
$_____. Please send my book(s) to :

Name _____
(please print)

Address _____

_____

Chapter 2

The Birth of Social Evolution

Biological evolution is still the major evolutionary force in all organisms on earth except Homo sapiens (human beings). Development to the level of the group was essential for all animals in order for mating and procreation to occur, allowing the species to survive and prosper. For all levels, too, the most general form of information flow is communication. All animals "talk" to each other and have "body language" rituals which convey messages to each other and help each organism to meet its survival needs.

However, the whole evolutionary scheme took on a new meaning with the appearance on earth of human beings. This special species of organism can not only process matter/energy to sustain our own functioning systems, but we also bring stored information (experience) into any situation we enter - which we can and do exchange with other human beings. Thus, in human beings, the group also provided the first opportunity for social evolution. All of the later living system levels - organizations, societies, and supranational systems - have evolved only with human beings and are a function of our ability to store and exchange information with each other - and to build on the experiences of other human beings to create new evolutionary potential.

So perhaps it's time we took a closer look at the special organisms called "people." Maybe we can learn some things about ourselves which will help us to recognize good choices. Let's start by looking at the way we communicate. Communication is the most widespread form of information flow in all living systems - including us - and is absolutely essential to allow social evolution to grow and prosper.

Speech seems to be a vital variable here - perhaps the most vital. But wait a minute. Babies require very good communication with their caregivers, particularly in their earliest growth and development, in order to survive. But both speech and how to use it to convey meaning have to be learned, and that takes a while. How do they bridge that important gap? Just like lower animals, they bridge it with "body language."

Each of us starts life with little or no practice in understanding and communicating our needs. But, of course, we get lots of practice right away because we have lots of needs to be satisfied. Except for relatively undifferentiated crying and gurgling (compared to later rich verbal output), our communications for the first few years are essentially nonverbal. We learn to perceive and interpret other people's body language - tone of voice and any other cues and signals we can pick up - to help us judge how they are reacting to us. And by responding with our own body language, tone of voice, etc. we let them know how we feel about it all.

Babies communicate with facial expressions, by the way they hold their bodies, and by cooing or crying. And parents become very alert to all the baby's signals that convey how it feels and what it needs. Since infants' very survival for the first few years depends on getting what they need from their caregivers (food, drink, diaper changes, hugs and kisses, relief from special aches, pains and discomforts), use of body language is the first and most important skill they learn. It is so well learned by the time we can use meaningful speech that we never forget it. And, of course, that learning also comes in handy later on when we become the caregivers.

Often we can tell when people don't really mean what they say because we're especially sensitive to their body language. We all started out as newborns - without any ability to speak words and phrases to get our needs met -and unable to understand the words and phrases of our parents or other caregivers. The first language we learned was body language, and paying attention to the body language of those people filling our needs allowed us to survive and prosper, so it's not surprising that we've never forgotten it.

As we grow up, we add words and phrases to our communication skills. Some of us get so good at talking, in fact, that we almost forget that the whole transaction must be a two-way street if real information is to be exchanged and acted upon. But even when we're poor at listening to what other people are saying - and most of us don't listen well -our early training usually kicks in, and we pick up on the non-verbal messages instead.

Perhaps you can see that unless the message you send is the message I get, we're both handicapped. I'm unlikely to respond in the way you expected, and you - thinking that I understood you - will not understand my response. Distortions which occur in sending and receiving messages increase the magnitude of our interpersonal gap (the distance between what you intend and the effect of your message on me).

Such distortions occur for a number of reasons. Sometimes, when we don't really mean what we say, we send double messages that conflict with each other. Our verbal message is what we think we should say, and our non-verbal message conveys what we really mean or feel. Since we all learned early in our lives to rely on nonverbal cues - body language - to interpret ambiguous situations, the unspoken message usually carries a lot of weight when we interpret what someone else is saying. In those cases, actions do speak louder than words. I guess the lesson here is "Let's all practice what we preach, and don't be afraid to trust your intuitions. They are often right."

Sometimes it is simply our style of delivery which leads to distortions in the message being received. Lecturers and scientists who read papers at meetings are notorious for making even the most exciting and vital information dull and unable to be interpreted. They mumble, use clinical jargon unfamiliar to the audience, or drone on in an expressionless monotone.

Perhaps the most powerful influences on our messages are the <u>internal filters</u> that we use both in sending and in receiving our communications. Among these are:

• our self image - our confidence, or lack of it.

• our image of the one receiving the communication - whether we think the person is friendly or hostile, or whether we view the person as wise or stupid.

• the purpose of the communication - whether we're courting someone or asking for directions.

• our vested interest in the outcome - how much we care, and why (suppose your grade or your job depends on what you say to me).

• our expectations about the outcome - influenced by our previous experience in similar situations.

As though all these message distorters were not enough, our language and our verbal culture can often be ambiguous. Different folks use different codes, largely based in their own previous learning and experiences. Many times I've listened to a couple of able scholars from closely related disciplines argue about their theories. All too often, the scientific jargon they use sounds the same but really means something slightly different to each of them. Each ends up at a loss to understand why the other can't see the logic of his or her explanation.

*   *   *   *   *

Whenever two or more people try to communicate with each other without realizing that they're using different meanings, there are more and more serious breakdowns in

28

communications - which even more firmly lock in our stereotypes about each other and interfere with our working together more effectively.

However, diversity of background skills and experience can be turned to advantage in a task-oriented group - if group members can learn to read each other's signals accurately. Then the group can become a viable problem-solving organism.

Since each of its body parts - the people in it - have different types of life experience to draw from, each can make unique contributions to the group's ability to take all relevant factors into account and to come up with workable solutions. Without good communication, problem-solving groups construct figurative "towers of Babel" with every worker speaking a different tongue and with little or no creative interaction possible.

We often express our feelings about others by labeling the people rather than describing the way we feel. Thus you might say "Maggie is certainly a dull writer' rather than "when I read what Maggie writes, I feel like dropping off to sleep." I might not seem dull at all to someone who is used to my jargon or vitally needs to understand what I'm writing about. And even you sleepyheads might be more turned on by what you're reading if you'd spent last night sleeping - instead of studying or partying. So sending our messages when we have an attentive receiver is also important. If you're really tired now, try reading this over when you've had some rest.

An important way to improve our skills in preventing and repairing breakdowns in communication is to become more effective listeners. The ability to listen well is at least as essential to good communication as the ability to express yourself well. Good listening is a process demanding alert and active participation. It requires that we hear the other's whole thought without interrupting, and that we concentrate on what she or he is trying to convey. It helps to be patient, open to considering what you're hearing as a way to understand more about the speaker, and to respond in ways which will encourage improved communication.

To get a feel for the usefulness of these concepts and to hone your skills for communicating, try describing them in your own words - using examples from your own experiences. You may be better able to realize that all these phenomena are often operating in your everyday interactions with your friends and associates. And just letting the speaker know that you don't understand what he or she means often improves communications. Unless you indicate otherwise, most of us automatically assume that you've gotten our message.

*   *   *   *   *

The survival needs of human babies also had a marked influence on the evolution of differences between males and females. This is also true in lower animals to some degree. It became more and more marked with the evolution of primates. As organisms become more complex, the newborn infant is unable to survive for longer and longer periods unless it has help to fill its nurturing needs and to protect it from the external threats in its world. In almost all animal species, females became the receptacles for receiving the seeds of the union between males and females, and for providing a home for the embryo's gestation until its birth.

It's not surprising then, as babies needed more and more looking after to survive after birth, that the mother became the major source of the looking after. It also seems quite natural that - in human and many subhuman species - the father assumed the role of provider for the new family. Without developing a clear definition of who took major responsibility for each of an infant's critical needs as it developed, those species almost certainly would not have survived and prospered. Thus, of necessity, Mom took care of the homestead while Pop did the

30

hunting, fishing, shelter building, and when necessary, fought off invaders.

Cultural shaping, like body language, is an example of "growing up socialization phenomena." These are activities and signals consistently taught to children to assure that the differences in roles and responsibilities for males and females are accepted and clearly understood by people in the culture. To the extent that a community is multiracial or multicultural, adult modeling of "appropriate behavior" in relation to racial or cultural differences is also growing up socialization behavior.

Over time, in our society, and in most other societies that I know about, little girls learned how to take care of children and keep house as they grew up, and in the process were socialized to be sensitive to the needs of others and where necessary, to care for them. Little boys learned skills appropriate to protectors and providers with emphasis on competition, being better at what they did than other little boys, particularly in sports. In short, males were expected to be useful while females were also expected to be helpful.

Those expectations produce different socialization processes for little girls and little boys. It's perhaps significant for the future of these two processes that while being useful is certainly a valuable trait, being helpful as well has the added characteristic of promoting some important ongoing processes of social evolution, like encouraging others to learn how to work together in harmony to get something done.

For males with aspirations to join with a woman and raise a family, and for females with aspirations to join with a man and raise a family, the traditional role assignments - made by our biological evolutionary process a hundred thousand years ago to assure survival of the species - often still work amazingly well. However, complications began to arise as social evolution in humans accelerated at a much faster pace than biological

31

evolution. Many of today's humans, both male and female, find those role assignments a very poor fit.

As a scientist, I've never taken much stock in labels, particularly when you're talking about human beings, female or male. Labels try to put folks in "one size fits all" categories, and we're much too diverse in the essence of our lives and life-styles for that to work. To me, the evidence supports the likelihood that gender is really a single continuum (or line graph) which has a bimodal distribution (two humps instead of one). We all start out with the same equipment in the womb. We all have some masculine and some feminine characteristics. The ratio of testosterone to estrogen hormones that we come with as embryos (influenced by the number of X and/or Y genes on our 23rd chromosomes) determines where we fall on that line graph.

Most males cluster under one hump (a bell shaped normal curve) and most females under the other. Some of us are somewhere between the two humps, and a few of us are at one or the other extreme of the graph. Though they are often a source of misunderstanding and strong emotions among us socially, I don't see why we need to fear or feel negative about our differences. Nature produces normal distributions in living systems all the time. Our differences are what makes life interesting. And we all have a right to be here and to be ourselves rather than somebody else's idea of what we should be. Diversity is a very important source of positive energy in the social evolution of the human organism. It plays a primary role in our growth and development as individuals.

*   *   *   *   *

It may be useful to pause here and realize that "sex" was created during the biological evolutionary process to provide DNA (gene) exchange at conception. Each parent contributes to the embryo one of the paired genes for each trait which the parent possesses. This insures that each offspring will get a mix

32

of characteristics from its two parent organisms that makes it a bit different than either parent. All organisms within a species have the same numbers and types of chromosomes; yet there is a wide diversity of traits within our subsystems (hair, eye color, skin color, height, weight, intelligence, etc.)

The science of genetics allows us to trace our mitochondrial DNA (and that of all other Homo sapiens) through our maternal lineage back to a few thousand inhabitants of Africa. All surviving human beings, all over the world, descended from migrants from that population. The recombination of traits, which occurs in the offspring of sexual reproduction, allows the emergence of new and useful features both within the species and across living system levels - while maintaining our evolutionary heritage. One important argument against human cloning involves the risks of losing that genetic variability in offspring with only one source of genetic inheritance.

You may have noticed that there's a new emphasis in child-rearing practices encouraging us to play music for, play with and read to our children regularly and often, starting at their birth and continuing into early childhood. Some experts suggest that we start playing music for and talking to the baby months before it is born. This emphasis grows out of recent discoveries that, in their earliest years, kids are already learning how to organize their worlds and are beginning to form the logical and emotional structures on which all of their later learning will be built. It also helps them to start learning the spoken language which they'll use for the rest of their lives.

These capabilities have always been there in human organisms but, as with other evolutionary characteristics, we had to discover and understand them before we could take fuller advantage of their existence. This particular discovery is already beginning to significantly affect the patterns of education in our homes and schools and the learning potentials of our children.

*   *   *   *   *

This is a good time to take a closer look at some of the ways in which social evolution makes people different from other organisms, and at the top of the list is communication: the most widespread form of information flow in all living systems. For other species, body language and relatively routine vocalizations are still the major means of sending messages to each other, even in pre-human primates. Homo sapiens is the only species still existing which is capable of the elaborate and diverse speech by which we exchange, retain, and build upon our own and others' ideas and discoveries.

The development of our <u>vocal apparatus</u> allowed us to create such speech patterns. With this apparatus, we can and do demonstrate our <u>neural potential</u> to achieve and retain learning which we can then share and exchange with others. The development of both <u>verbal capacity</u> and <u>neural capability</u> were events of <u>biological evolution</u>. But they provided the underpinnings for <u>social evolution</u> to take off beyond the "group" stage.

We began building extended families, then collections of separate families with common needs and goals, which we now call communities. Communities found within themselves the potential for linking people with specialized skills into even more complex organizations offering specialized services. Large communities became cities that collected together into states, and then nations — which are societies with common written and spoken languages.

Early on, it must have been apparent that speech limited us to face-to-face communication, so we invented drawings, symbols and written language, along with systems to exchange them over longer and longer distances. Our latest invention, the Internet, also permits communication across societies with

34

different languages and customs. A good thing it does, too, as it greatly enhances the ability of people in our supranational systems to communicate across and among international borders.

However, it is also true that social evolution still has a long way to go before our supranational systems (NATO and the United Nations, for example) have <u>fully integrated decider processes</u> (leadership decision making capabilities) as well as <u>widely recognized and respected power</u> to allow them to function smoothly and consistently in pursuing the goals of their component subsystems (our nations).

*   *   *   *   *

Living "another way" - as this book proposes - requires that we emphasize looking for and building on existing assets of whatever level of living system is socially evolving - rather than exacting punishments or revenge for its deficits. Because time only moves in a forward direction, we can never go back and fix something which has already occurred, So backward-focused retribution squanders our energy and creates negative and destructive forces amongst us. The first step is to learn from our failures, so we recognize that change is imperative. Then include all participants in planning for and building on assets which predict success.

This is true whether it be in our personal lives or in the systems of justice that we enact and enforce at state, national, and international levels. Whatever is wrong and needs to be changed should prompt us to look for new solutions, so the problems don't recur, rather than wasting our energies on punishing whoever was involved in the non-functional mistake. However, it's particularly important that <u>they</u> learn the new, more functional solutions, so they don't repeat the non-productive errors.

In a democracy, laws only work when they reflect the will and understanding of the people in the communities in which they are applied. In such cases, the integrity of the community itself requires that such laws be consistent and effective over time. When the community either doesn't believe in them or doesn't understand why they are valuable, they will be honored most often by finding ways around them or ignoring them whenever possible.

Thus, if something isn't working, we should look for why it isn't working and get people involved in devising other solutions which will work better. When this happens, "acceptable behavior' is newly defined and becomes clearer to and better supported by the target population. Only then should we pass laws—to clarify and enforce the desired behavior and to assure our common understanding of what's expected of us and why.

One good intention that figuratively paved the road to hell involves the evolution of seat belts as an important assist in making us safer in our cars when accidents occur. Probably because they work well in race cars and airplanes, auto makers developed and installed seat belts in the cars and trucks that we drive every day, and law enforcement folks began lengthy and elaborate campaigns to get people to wear them. However, they neglected the small detail that the seat belts were designed as though we were all the size of the average man. For many drivers and passengers, these harnesses were, and often still are, very uncomfortable to wear. Thus, in addition to our human reluctance to change well-established unconstrained driving habits, we had a built-in excuse not to use them, since they choked many of us and didn't fit well.

Fortunately, the driving population is becoming more aware that seat belts really do save lives, and some improvements have been made in their design. Also, since semi trucks, SUV's, sedans, and VW bugs share the same overused lanes of our driving spaces, the obvious reality that highways are becoming less and less safe has accented the urgency of universal seat belt enforcement.

Drivers in some states have finally accepted a law making driving without fastening our seat belts illegal, and we've developed special restraints for babies and young kids. The fact that more drivers and passengers now voluntarily comply helps make more rigorous enforcement of the law more effective, and the percentage of travelers who buckle up has improved markedly.

*   *   *   *   *

To improve the effectiveness of our justice systems, we must not only learn what we want the outcomes of legal processes to accomplish. We must also design ways to successfully get from here to there. Our present criminal justice systems emphasize finding out who is to blame and deciding how to punish them and/or how or what they should pay for what they have done.

The most likely outcome is that they will be sent to prison for varying lengths of time, living with other criminals in cages. This is also supposed to protect the rest of us from any further threat from them. It's true that this may keep them off the streets until they have served their time. But it can hardly be expected to improve their social skills so they'll fit better in our communities when they are released. Maybe, while they are in our institutions, our first step should be to help them learn more productive ways to live successfully, so they have a better chance to become productive citizens when they get out. Each time we succeed in accomplishing this, we all win.

Chapter 3

Why We Care

The biological evolution of Homo sapiens - the only surviving human species - was pretty much completed over 100,000 years ago. Neanderthal humans apparently lived during the early period of human development, but they did not survive over time as a species. Our bodies still respond much as they did then, even though the world of today is much more complex and makes many very different demands on us. We still need constant access to oxygen, water, heat, and nourishment within specific and predictable amounts in order to live and grow. Though we often act as though it weren't so, our bodies also need regular rest and sleep in predictable amounts to keep them in homeostatic balance.

Over the ages, we have come to vary markedly in shapes, sizes, and skin color as a function of where and how we grew up, but we all start out with basically the same equipment that we had from the time the species originated - a head with one nose and two eyes and ears, two arms and legs, and the same internal organs, all run by our very special brains. Doctors trained in the United States can and do treat people anywhere in the world and deal with essentially the same physiological and anatomic features.

Our main blessing - and sometimes our problem - seems to be the tremendous potential of our brains to create and develop our minds. As has been amply demonstrated repeatedly during human history throughout the world, human beings are capable of, and have occasionally achieved either the heights of compassionate morality and integrity - or the depths of violent and reprehensible destruction - using those same awesome brains. How come?

As far as science has been able to determine, it's mostly because we remember and learn from our life experiences and from each other as we mature. In the process, we develop value systems which influence who we become. Every day, each one of us meets life situations which call for thought, opinion, decision, and action. Such situations may be more or less important to us and more or less familiar to us, but every decision we make and every action we take is based on the beliefs, attitudes, and values that we hold.

At every turn, we are forced to make choices about how to live our lives. Many times, these choices must be made in the face of conflicting or confused notions about what would be best. How often during the last month have you wondered what or who was "right" in a conflict about one of more of the following areas?

politics	religion	money	health	work
school	friends	family	love	sex
culture	race	hobbies	rules	property

All of us, young or old, become confused about our values at times. We are surrounded by alternative points of view, frequently espoused by people whom we respect equally - or nearly so - although perhaps for different reasons. How, in this morass of conflict and confusion, do we tell what the "right" choice is? How do we learn to understand and feel good about the decisions we do make? How can we respect and cooperate with people who believe differently?

It may help us to explore both our own beliefs and those of others if we focus on the process of valuing rather than the content of specific values. In other words, how do we come to hold certain beliefs and establish certain behavior patterns? Let's start with a definition. What do we mean by "values"?

A value is a characteristic or an attribute of some general area of human experience which is considered desirable by an individual or by a group. It's usually expressed in positive terms about a general class of things, and It serves as a base for decisions about specifics within that class. Values may range in significance from those which serve as a moral creed to live by (It is wrong to cheat other people) to those which influence our decisions about quite mundane matters (chocolate or strawberry ice cream for dessert?).

When we were very young, we became aware of which things were important to us - in choosing our friends, buying a toy, watching a TV show, or joining our friends in a game after school. As we matured, "things important to us" became values which generalize to a class of behaviors to which they apply. Thus, if we value "friendliness," we may feel good about friendly teachers, friendly dogs, and friendly neighbors. But how do such things become important to us?

As growing children, we observe and interact with family members and people outside the family, becoming aware of what others expect of us. This awareness of expectations serves as a set of ground rules which we use to decide how we should respond to the different kinds of situations in which we find ourselves. As we mature and gain experience, we also become better able to conceptualize value. This allows us to begin to sort out and, to some extent, to pick and choose our own values, as distinct from those of our parents, teachers, or friends.

As you might expect, many of our values as adults closely resemble those of our parents, and some closely resemble those of our friends. We call this acculturation. It's partly an outcome of the personal reinforcement we receive when we agree with others whom we respect or care about. It's also partly because we're more comfortable with people who think like we do, so we unconsciously gravitate toward such folks for our friends and teachers.

This tendency in all of us can become almost a prison for some of us. To the extent that we can't enjoy and learn from people who believe differently than we do or hold different values, we limit our own ability to encounter new viewpoints and sample the exciting diversity which exists in human life styles and living experiences. Since we're all limited by our own life experiences, our growth is often enhanced by such encounters when they allow us to expand our repertoire of possible points of view.

*   *   *   *   *

You may have heard "life" described as "a state of being." As I suggested earlier, I prefer the more dynamic statement that "living is a process of becoming." We are all constantly changing. It is the nature of living systems to change. We change physiologically, we change emotionally, and we also change spiritually. That is, our beliefs and values change. The codes that we live by change, and as a result of those changes, our behavior, the way we live, changes.

This holds true not only for individuals, but also for our groups, organizations, societies, and supranational systems. Of course, the more complex the system, the longer it takes for major changes to occur. This may not surprise you, since all the higher level systems, from the group on, are made up of individual people, and the more of us there are, the harder it is to get us to adopt common values. Later, we'll look at the ways in which leaders try to influence this process as social evolution proceeds.

As our individual values become more firmly grounded, they are less susceptible to change. We perceive that actions

42

consistent with our values not only yield positive outcomes but also are like the values of those we respect or admire. They also tend to agree with the values of our culture, so we feel a sense of personal integrity and self worth which enhances and reinforces those values.

When we perceive that actions consistent with our values yield negative outcomes, are not consistent with the values of those we respect or admire, or don't agree with the values of our culture, such values give rise to tensions which cause us to reexamine and possibly modify or change them. For instance, when I get terribly upset or defensive over someone else's arguments or behavior, I have learned to stop short and ask myself why it upsets me so. It usually turns out that they have reminded me of an aspect of myself that I don't really like, or of a conflict in my own values that I haven't yet resolved.

Values are neither actions per se nor judgments. They are the basis for such actions and judgments. Thus we need to move beyond recognizing that our actions and our judgments are determined by our basic values. We also need to identify and become aware of the specific values which determine those actions and judgments.

Healthy valuing, then, involves prizing and cherishing our beliefs and behaviours and publicly affirming those beliefs and behaviours when appropriate. It also involves choosing those beliefs and behaviours from available alternatives after consideration of the consequences of such choices for our self-images and for our future growth. Then we can comfortably act on our beliefs regularly and consistently.

It is also possible to infer the values of others from what they say and do. As we get to know our friends and associates, we develop stereotypes about what they value and believe. If we stop listening to each other and stop observing the ways in which, while we have been growing and changing, our friends

43

have also been maturing, we may some day be surprised to discover how much <u>they</u> have changed. Perhaps it's useful, now and then to take another look.

*   *   *   *   *

Just as our search for our own values is facilitated by a supportive and accepting environment, we should respect other people's right to hold different opinions and to act in accordance with their different convictions. It is useful to try to understand - and to accept as valid - different viewpoints, though that does <u>not</u> require that we agree with them.

As individuals in problem-solving groups, we sometimes find ourselves becoming defensive about our values for reasons which are not always clear. Most of the time, this is because we perceive, sometimes accurately, that others' questions about our values are oriented toward personal threat or attack. Often we tie the ideas, thoughts, or suggestions of either ourselves or others to the persons expressing the ideas, thoughts, or suggestions, in such a way as to make the person and the idea inseparable. Thus we listen to what is being said only in terms of our feelings about the person saying it, rather than in terms of the content of the thought being expressed.

When we do this, we distort an important part of the message being received. This seriously interferes with the communication process and sets up a climate for personal attack rather than mutual exploration. This has important implications for group interactions as well as personal relationships. We always bring our personal values to any group In which we participate. So do other members of the group. Some of these values are bound to be different, though not all of the differences will be relevant to the group's purpose.

For example, our country has two major political parties. Sometimes members search for reasons to criticize candidates from the 'other' party and to praise candidates from their own - rather than debating about what needs to be done and which candidate is best equipped to do it. And sometimes we don't think much about issues. We vote for the most 'likeable' candidate, regardless of his or her skills.

*   *   *   *   *

Every group, of course, develops group values. These include norms about what behaviours are appropriate in the group, as well as the agreed upon goals for the group to accomplish - which ordinarily define its reason for existence. When group objectives are made explicit and set with an understanding of their relationship to the individual goals which members bring with them to the group, intragroup conflict will be minimal and intragroup respect and dedication to the group's purpose will be maximal.

Provided members are primarily concerned with the group's mission and how it functions to achieve that mission, value differences which are not relevant to the group's goals can be ignored. Individual value differences which are relevant to group purposes, however, must be recognized and dealt with if the group is to remain viable and functional. People who do not feel personally vulnerable or defensive and who can hear other group members in terms of the content and relevance of their expressions rather than in terms of their personal characteristics stand the best chance of dealing non-defensively with - and of resolving satisfactorily - important value differences within the group. This is one of the primary functions of a group facilitator, by the way.

*   *   *   *   *

Our abilities to learn from experience and to share our findings with each other are the main keys to why we have moved so quickly into the benefits and problems of social evolution.

The major benefit is that we can use the combined experiences of all participants to build our creations and to find solutions to our problems. For this to happen, however, clear, mutually understood communication between and among us is crucial. The larger the group, the harder this is to pull off.

If you think about it, you may realize that the person you communicate with most effectively is always yourself. You're more likely than anyone else to know how you feel and what you want. And those two factors are the major determinants of the way each of us behaves. The better you know someone else, the more likely that you will understand each other when you interact, so two person exchanges are often quite successful, especially if we know the person well. As more than two people become involved, however, all of whom have different life experiences and value sets, the task of thinking and working together gets harder.

As humans developed higher levels of social evolution, like groups, organizations, societies and supranational systems, these bodies needed to build more complex networks to support their subsystems. Growing populations and industrialization increased the interdependency both within and across systems. In addition, the concurrent growth of other groups, organizations, societies, and supranational systems - often in competition for the same resources - introduced conflict between the competing bodies and reduced the freedom of each system to unrestrained growth and development of its creative potential.

Modern organizations, societies, and supranational systems are highly vulnerable to such disruption. Yet they are expected to provide more services to their subsystems (i.e. individuals, families, and other social groups) and to control more social variables (like justice and personal welfare) than earlier, less evolved systems were expected to do. It should be apparent, when you think about it, that we still have a lot to learn about how to do this effectively, though we're much better at it than we used to be - if you look far enough back in our history.

*   *   *   *   *

One important variable which evolved with social evolution is money. The flow of money as a special form of communication has, since its invention, been very important to our species both within and between levels of living systems. This has not been an unmixed blessing, depending on whether money is used as a medium of exchange to acquire needed resources and services - or as an instrument to exert power and control by the possessor over individuals or other subsystems.

Some folks put so much emphasis on the acquisition of wealth that it becomes an end in itself. This has given money a bad name. However, remember that the old saying goes "the love of money is the root of all evil" which suggests that it's the way we feel about it that gets us into trouble.

Just as money can be used either to acquire needed resources and services or to exert power and control over others, advertising is useful when it is structured to help us find resources or information that we need. However when marketing tries to convince us that we need what someone else wants to sell us - whether we actually need it or not - it becomes another example of exerting control over others to one's own advantage. We see examples of this much too frequently in telemarketing, television, and radio commercials.

The use of public media to gain or maintain power and control is well exemplified in our political systems whenever members of our executive and legislative branches must spend more time and effort raising money to get reelected than they do creating our laws or running our government. It illustrates a very dangerous strategy - often defended by claiming that the ends justify the means. Thus, the party which can afford to pay

47

for more media exposure gets more of its members elected. They then have a better chance of influencing the creation of our laws and the conduct of our government, regardless of whether their candidates have the best skills and experience to do those jobs.

Such strategies always compromise the integrity of the systems to which they are applied. They upset the homeostatic balance among the participants in the system by giving temporary advantage to those applying them. If we, as citizens in our democracy, want our leaders and representatives to come up with solutions which work best for all of us, they must be able to think together and build on each others' ideas to accomplish such outcomes.

Strategies which foster competition rather than collaboration between political parties reduce our ability to effectively tap into multi-group reservoirs of richly varied life experiences. Access to these reservoirs is what enables human beings to develop more insightful solutions which better accommodate all of us. When we continue to use old compromises which have worked poorly in the past, deluding ourselves that we can't do better, we risk further degradation of both our cultural heritage and the furthering of social evolution. If our competitive energies are directed toward beating down opposing points of view which are interfering with achieving our own party's agenda, creative collaboration simply won't occur. All of us, who must live within the laws and governing policies that result, are the ultimate losers.

When only thirty to fifty percent of us vote in our elections, and not everyone is adequately informed about the issues in question, entropy is already beginning to threaten the survival of our living system. We'd better be willing to insist that our leaders design voting strategies which insure that all of our votes are counted when we do vote. And we'd better start educating ourselves, our fellow citizens, and particularly our kids about how each of us can nurture and protect the democracy that we're so proud of - if we don't want to lose it!

*   *   *   *   *

The above example also illustrates another mixed blessing about our species called <u>human adaptability</u>. Without it, we would not have been able to move over the whole earth with all of its geological variability. We survived threatening changes in climate and living conditions by inventing new non-living systems or adapting available plants and animals to supply needed protections. Thus we have met life-threatening challenges and have provided the matter/energy resources with which we continue to grow and prosper.

However, this same human adaptability, with all of its inherent flexibility, sometimes allows us to adapt to - and to put up with - almost anything that occurs in human relationships. Even though we may recognize inappropriate behavior of a person, a group, an organization, or a society, if we don't have a solution available, we often simply deny that the problem exists - or find someone to blame for it, without taking steps to develop better solutions. The more this happens, the harder it is to change things. The longer we wait, the more likely the end result will be some kind of violence, either to us or by us or both.

Wars between nations are prime examples of this. There are no winners in war or any other violence. Everybody loses eventually, though that may not be apparent at the time that one side claims victory. War never brings peace. It only sets up circumstances and motivations in which new peace-oriented collaborations <u>can</u> occur.

The apparent victors must actively help the defeated entity to restructure its system into one which is socially and economically viable both for it and for the community of nations with which it interacts. A part of this help must focus on recovery

49

by all participants from the social and economic devastation which inevitably accompanies the conflict.

Such actions improve the possibility that overall <u>social homeostasis</u> (the ability to keep all important variables in the system in balance over time) will result among the participant nations. They may then be able to establish peaceful coexistence in the only world that we all inhabit! Just as physiological homeostasis is necessary for survival and growth of all levels of living systems, social homeostasis is crucial for harmonious relations to prevail among the human beings living and interacting within and among all participating nations.

We did accomplish this after the Second World War, in fact, in both the European and the Pacific theatres. The victorious allied nations worked together through the Allied Control Commission and the newly chartered United Nations to guide both Germany and Japan through the establishment of peacefully elected assemblies and eventual membership in the United Nations. <u>Today, over fifty years later, they are both independent nations, contributing economically and socially to global stability.</u>

Apparently, they are also comfortable enough with their own emergent identities to sometimes question some of our actions. This means that we did most of that World War 11 job of reestablishing balance among our nations pretty well.

As we begin a new century ringing with violent threats of several varieties which have semi-global dimensions, perhaps we need to look more closely at the positive solutions which history can suggest. The ones that work always include mutual trust and respect as well as working together to achieve win-win outcomes for all parties involved. Creative cultural growth in multilevel complex systems flourishes when members at all levels of organization share both opportunities for meaningful inputs and benefits from successful functioning.

And we must recognize that the advantages that our complex systems bring to us will be accompanied by new threats and problems. We need to face these together, and address them in ways that foster socially homeostatic balance. Pretending that they don't exist won't make them go away.

Chapter 4

Exploring Family Functions

Since our initial exposure to social evolution almost always occurs in one or more family groups, it's useful to examine their nature and their function more closely. It was from observing and interacting with family members, usually your birth or <u>nuclear family</u> that you received the essentials for your own survival in your first few years. Your nuclear family consisted of you, your parents, your brothers and sisters, if any, and often included surviving grandparents.

One or more of them provided you with food, drink, comfort needs, and, hopefully, your first post-birth exposures to warmth, affection, and safety from various threats. You also had lots of opportunities to hone your skills at using body language until you learned how to verbalize (speak to communicate) your needs and thoughts more effectively.

As you tried to find your way around this brand new world, so different from your mother's womb, your behavior may occasionally have either alarmed or annoyed one or more of those family members. In their efforts to control your explorations, they may have been the source of your first reinforced feelings of alarm and fear when they sharply reprimanded you - perhaps even spanked you -to communicate their disapproval of what you were doing.

You may also have picked up the harmonies and dissonances in their body language as they interacted with each other, when their voices held tones of gentleness, irritation, or threat. What we learn during those first few years helps to determine our emotional foundations as we move into the world of interpersonal relationships in our growth toward maturity.

The nuclear family serves as the hub for functions involving the growth and development of participating members. We usually think of this in relation to the children in the family, but it really begins with the union of their parents - and the establishment of their common home. Getting used to living with each other's habits and biases and learning to understand each other's messages often takes a while. Success in their ability to work toward common goals and support each other's efforts predicts that the marriage will contribute to each partner's emotional maturation, as well as to the emotional health of the offspring once they appear. Perhaps it's a good thing that gestation takes nine months, another of Mother Nature's wisdoms.

Maturation of individuals within human families is influenced by both biogenic and sociogenic forces during our lives. These forces will have differential effects on different family members depending on the developmental stage of each member when they occur. In the womb, the embryo receives all of its oxygen and its nutrients from its mother via her blood vessels as they course through its home in the placenta. During the gestation period, the embryo shares everything that its mother eats, drinks, or breathes.

The developing embryo is also affected by biochemical secretions in its mother's blood stream either from medications or from strong emotional experiences both positive and negative. This is why pregnant women so frequently are cautioned about substances they put into their bodies. For instance, alcoholic beverages, ingested while pregnant, go full strength directly through the placenta and surround the embryo. Since alcohol Is terotogenic (very destructive) to nervous tissue, serious harm can result to the developing fetus.

Fetal Alcohol Spectrum Disorder (FASD) is the most severe manifestation of such neural damage, showing up in babies after they are born and affecting them for the rest of their lives. Expectant mothers totally prevent the development of FASD in their babies when they abstain from drinking alcohol while pregnant.

Proper nutrition is important at all ages, but it's most critical in children because of the accelerated rate at which their bodies grow and mature. At the same time, they are coping with new challenges to their self-images as they meet and interact with teachers and other people outside their nuclear family. Having consistent warm acceptance from parents and siblings makes exploring a sometimes threatening outside world a lot less scary for kids - and enhances their ability to find their own place in that world.

Forces which disrupt the homeostatic harmonies of the nuclear family, such as domestic violence and/or divorce of the parents, are scarier and more threatening for their children than for the parents. The youngsters need the security of family harmony as they try out new experiences. Most often, when things go wrong, they assume that it's somehow their fault, and adults in the turmoil of discord or separation are often unaware of this.

As young people mature, consistent experiences as part of warm and supportive nuclear families also provide models which help them to establish their own harmonious nuclear families when they become adults. Family systems are especially important for teens to use as models when they begin making some of their own decisions as they move into non-family relationships.

By now, they're beginning to value their own independence. Good models of how we can help ourselves to achieve what we want and need - while respecting the efforts of others to do likewise - are crucial to teen development. Mistakes can be valuable learning experiences when both the teen and other family members emphasize experimenting with creative solutions rather than focusing only on blame or guilt about making the mistake.

It's Important to firmly identify and try to prevent recurrence of hurtful and/or violent behavior without incurring feelings of guilt in the teen. Such feelings get In the way of effective learning. But intrafamily collaboration in addressing family problems and dysfunctions provides young people with practice in "getting along" - in preparation for the time when collaboration with others in one's community becomes necessary and desirable. And, of course, as young adults look toward establishing lasting marital companionships in which to nourish new nuclear families of their own, they have a real head start if they have learned this skill while they were growing up.

*   *   *   *   *

One of the better examples of social evolution in action, by the way, is the <u>extended family,</u> usually consisting of relatives and/or very close friends. It insures that there will be others to back up the primary caregivers when they need support both to assure safety and to enforce family discipline. Thus in the recent past and - though more rarely - sometimes even now in some small towns and long-established neighborhoods, relatives and neighbors kept an eye on youngsters in transit from home to school - then to after school activities and back home again.

Often, if a child got into a fight or other trouble during that trek, the primary caregiver knew about it before the young offender reached home. And when older family members needed additional support as they aged and/or became infirm, the extended family shared in looking after them, too. Unfortunately, modern living has put the extended family in jeopardy of disappearing into history without developing an effective replacement.

These days, many members move away from the family home as they get married, find jobs elsewhere, go off to centers of higher education, or simply set out to explore a much more accessible world. With the frequency of out-of-wedlock childbirth and early divorce increasing, extended family safety nets are becoming quite rare. Young mothers often find themselves without the assists we used to have in learning how to raise children. When it's necessary for the mother to work away from home, finding resources to care for them is often difficult, if not impossible. Unfortunately, more and more, even in intact marital homes, both parents need to work outside the home to meet family expenses.

Governmental agencies provide substitutes (i.e. welfare, social services, day care centers, foster homes, nursing homes, and particularly our schools) to help isolated family subgroups in trouble. However, our institutions are still a long way from dealing effectively with events which the naturally evolved extended family used to handle routinely.

*   *   *   *   *

As the tempo of our cultural interactions accelerates, the gap in resources available to the wealthiest and the poorest of our families grows ever larger. And the contrast between health and educational opportunities open to rich and poor children growing up in our communities gets more marked and harder to ignore politically. The way our governmental bodies are presently organized often means that well-off people in power try to provide solutions to correct such inequities. But however sincerely they want to do the job, their own life experiences have seldom equipped them to offer solutions which work for folks who are trying to survive with very limited resources. Thus they usually fail to create insightful systems which really meet the needs of families who can't pay for privilege and the inequities continue, though sometimes in slightly different form.

Perhaps this is a good time to consider the difference between <u>interdependent</u> and <u>codependent</u> relationships. Interdependent relationships grow out of our recognition that working together with one or more other people or groups to address common goals allows common access to the resources, knowledge and companionship of all participants in order to better achieve those goals. Interdependent relationships are built on mutual respect and clear, honest communication, and they benefit all who join in them. They are crucial components of healthy, harmonious nuclear families.

In contrast, codependency arises when one or more participants sacrifice their own rights and needs to maintain an ongoing dysfunctional relationship. A familiar example occurs when one or both parents don't play their parental roles adequately, and an older child in the family takes over parenting of the younger siblings - and sometimes of one or both parents as well. Another prime example of codependency occurs when one spouse is regularly violently abused by the other spouse, yet they stay together within the marriage.

*   *   *   *   *

In Chapter 2, I mentioned that cultural shaping over time developed strong mores or customs about appropriate roles of women and men in assuring the biological survival of our species. As social evolution has progressed, however, individual differences within both sexes have made these arbitrary male - female role assignments more and more problematic for a large number of our citizens. In addition, as human populations have grown over time, biological survival of our species no longer requires that every human being produce progeny.

The genetic wiring for Homo sapiens allows for a lot of flexibility in our social behavior. Our advanced brains allow us to make choices about how we fulfill our destinies, and many of

58

us establish other lifestyles than the traditional nuclear family. Some members of both sexes remain single, choosing to dedicate their energies more or less exclusively to career building or public service missions. Others link up with same-sex partners. These alternative lifestyles sometimes include raising children, often by adopting youngsters who have lost their own nuclear families.

Role reversals occur in other species as well, but they are rare and seldom optional since they are biologically wired into the behavioral patterns of the whole species. For example, in a few species of birds, the female does the courting and chooses the male, who then incubates the eggs which she lays in a nest which he prepares. These behaviors, genetically wired into the species, don't allow them to choose any other way to conduct their courtships. They all do it this way.

Our ability to choose the way we will act in each situation we encounter is an important part of what makes human potential so much more dynamic than that of other species. It is entirely consistent with social evolution that, as human beings meet new challenges to traditional ways of living, some of us will try out new models which seem to make our lives more meaningful. Those models that work will persist. Those that don't will disappear. What is certain is that we'll each have opportunities to make choices as we mature, and for each of us, the task is to make choices that give meaning to our own particular lives. In the long run, each of us must do this for ourselves, and the choices we make will determine our satisfaction with the lives we live.

Chapter 5

Let's Get Organized

Having examined individuals and how they fit into families, it's time we looked at the composition and functions of the many systems outside the family with whom we are likely to interact throughout our lives. For young folks, the major ones are schools and religious institutions and, as with our families, the emphasis is still on each individual's needs and learning opportunities.

However, these systems also need to function well for everyone else in the group (the other stakeholders) if they are to continue to meet our needs. In this case, the other stakeholders include the students, teachers, administrators, and other school personnel as well as clergy, church personnel, and congregations. Once we're out of school - and sometimes while we're still there - we'll most likely enter the workplace where the primary focus becomes the way we function as groups in accomplishing the goals of the organization. As we do this, we need to consider not only what's good for ourselves, but for others in the organization and for the system as a whole.

Any social system consists of a collection of individual members. In healthy, well-functioning systems, members both trust and respect other members. They've also arrived at common goals for the organization - as well as a common understanding of why those goals are important to each of them - and how they'll try to reach them. When group values don't conflict with members' personal values, and if members understand each other reasonably well, working together should allow them to meet the organization's goals more quickly and more fully.

As we move outside of family circles, we will usually be involved with two major types of organizations - public and private. To survive, all organizations need regular sources of income to cover their expenses (offices, employees' salaries, etc.). Public institutions are most often non-profit. The funds they receive go exclusively to accomplish the goals and functions of the institution. Our governmental units at all levels (city, county, state, regional, and federal) are public, non-profit organizations. They're usually supported by taxes collected from their citizens.

Private organizations collect fees from consumers of their goods and services. Some of the incoming funds are redistributed as profit to the shareholders of the company and/or as bonuses to employees. In the United States, schools and health care organizations, including health maintenance organizations (HMO's), may be either public or private institutions, but they all collect fees for their services from some source.

Children are required to attend a public school supported by their state government unless their families can afford a private school. Many schools, as well as some health care services, are available only to people who can afford to pay for them. In many foreign countries, both educational and health services are provided by the national government without charge - as a right of citizenship. This reflects an implicit understanding that well-educated healthy citizens contribute to the ongoing soundness of the whole nation.

*   *   *   *   *

Most organizations, both public and private, function at more than one level of responsibility. Local, state, regional and national levels each perform somewhat different functions. Each needs to tackle different parts of the issues to be addressed, or the programs to be developed and executed. This adds two new complications to effectively building on each others' ideas and sharing relevant experiences to produce plans that work. The first is to adequately communicate between and among levels.

The second is to <u>agree</u> on which level should take responsibility for which functions.

For instance, local school boards are closest to the community and are most likely to know the number, types, and locations of schools and teachers which their students need. They have ready access to input from community residents about how the system is working and how the educational needs of their young charges are being satisfied or neglected.

However, to get the funds and other resources to accomplish these tasks usually means that they need support from their state department of education, which, in turn, gets its money from the state legislature. Each of these systems operate on budgets which they must justify to the sources of their funds (often state taxes, the Congress or the federal treasury). Poor communication among any of these may result in inadequate funding and consequent shortages in their operations.

While it's entirely appropriate for the higher level governmental funding sources to monitor how the local body spends its money, it is the funders' responsibility to fund the programs, <u>not to develop them or to run them.</u> The further removed they are from the programs they're funding, the less first-hand information they will have on which to base their decisions. Local boards need to keep governmental funding sources well informed about the valuable resources and services that the schools provide to their communities and the costs they incur in providing these services.

The state department of education is responsible for statewide educational policies and procedures. However, local communities under its jurisdiction vary broadly. Decisions about how its policies and procedures are carried out in each district usually are best made by the local schools. Local boards should regularly report to their state education department about the effects of their programs on students' knowledge and learning skills as well as their social maturation - and the resultant satisfaction or complaints of community residents.

*   *   *   *   *

Making choices in such complicated situations means distinguishing between selfishness and enlightened self-interest. Considering only ourselves in making our choices leaves out the needs of the rest of the system. That's what we mean by <u>selfishness</u>. If everyone does this, the assorted preferences of all the individuals involved will assure that opposing camps will most likely quarrel and create discord - increasing the amount of entropy in the system. This threatens the creative energy of the organization. Instead of trust and respect for each other, members feel a need to defend their own positions. Under these conditions, sharing ideas and building on each others' creativity becomes unlikely, if not impossible.

With <u>enlightened self-interest</u> we realize that it's to our advantage to keep the organization healthy so it can meet our needs - particularly when individual members have only limited resources. So we try to make our choices in ways that make sharing resources and building together more likely. This is sometimes called playing "win-win" games. Usually no one gets everything they want, but every participant comes away with something positive, and all can live with the decisions made.

This may not sound like many of the organizations that we experience today where job competition and turf protection seem to be paramount. Their organizational structure is usually a <u>patriarchal hierarchy</u>. That's a fancy way of saying that they are "top down" organizations where decisions are almost always made by a few powerful men who are in charge. In such organizations, cooperation often means "you coo, and I'll operate!"

64

Such hierarchies occur in both public and private organizations. They also form the basis both historically and currently for empires and dynasties. Their activities emphasize benefits to the leaders - to be supplied by the efforts of the people under their control. Special privileges are allotted to the empire's upper classes and/or to family members of the dynasty.

Wars are common in the histories of dynasties and empires. Instead of fostering collaborative sharing and trust among their peoples, they breed discontent, fear and mistrust - because the people seldom share in the rewards and privileges that winning the war may bring to their leaders.

All wars are conducted under hierarchical structures. The leaders send their warriors into battle to destroy opposing forces that stand in the way of the leaders' control over behavior of the enemy, often at great sacrifice to the warriors and their families. The death, destruction and widespread confusion that inevitably occur to warriors on both sides are considered a necessary evil to achieve the leaders' goals.

In hierarchical organizations, employees below the top levels have little opportunity for additional training, personal promotions, or significant input into planning. The prevailing view is often that the ends justify the means, even if you sacrifice a value or two. And every time someone wins, somebody else has to lose. This is often called "zero-sum" games.

As you might expect, in hierarchical systems there is little real communication, mutual respect, and trust. The inevitable result when such a group works on a common problem reminds me of the story about five people who were blindfolded and asked to examine and then describe an elephant. Of course they each produced a different description, depending on which part of the elephant they examined. And they clearly were not equipped to agree on what an elephant looks like.

So, how do we create effective, healthy organizations? Let's think back to our earlier discussion: why it's so hard to create social change. Organizations, like groups, societies, and supranational systems, are all made up of individuals. Societies and supranational systems, by their nature, also contain lots of groups and other organizations of assorted types and sizes. For all of them, it's just as true that the larger the number of people involved, the harder it is to get everyone to agree to the same goals and to accept the same solutions.

Smoothly operating organizations practice <u>team management</u> to achieve their success. They create and share common signals and common understandings about the nature and functions of the organization. They have well established and agreed upon procedures and strategies, and members understand their own roles and how they relate to the roles of others in the organization. Their organizational charts indicate who does what and who reports to whom. And all members have opportunities for regular inputs about the operation of their own work sites. The development of partnerships and collaborations within such systems provides opportunities to change zero-sum games into win-win games for everyone.

The same general rules apply for both public institutions and private companies. Their leaders must make a choice between establishing <u>top down power and control</u> or <u>team management throughout the organization</u>. As we saw in Chapter 1, in the last few years, we have seen corporations go bankrupt, their leaders jailed in disgrace, and many of their employees and shareholders go broke - after many years of "top down" hierarchical management strategies. Social evolution is never in a hurry to clearly show us our mistakes, but now that we have seen them, hopefully we can learn from them.

*   *   *   *   *

It helps to remember that most discoveries in scientific history happened when investigators who were looking for something else stumbled upon and recognized the significance of an outcome which was neither planned for nor expected. We call this <u>serendipity</u>, and the dictionary describes it as "the gift of finding valuable or agreeable things not sought for." It's most likely to occur when we approach our investigations with an open mind. Organizational leaders, as well as those involved in teaching and research (who should regularly be included in both commercial and educational systems), are more likely to experience serendipity in their operations when the prevailing atmosphere fosters open-minded sharing of ideas. It seems obvious that this will happen more often with team management than with hierarchies.

The advent of electronic technology to collect and measure data about what we do and how it affects our desired outcomes allows us to get periodic feedback to improve our systems and move them in the direction we want them to go. Good data can test the truth of early conclusions about what's going on. Old adages which persist over time are also a type of long duration research which contains "tried and true" potentials for discovering and understanding what's valuable, particularly in human interactions.

*   *   *   *   *

Let's take a moment to examine some of the characteristics which are most useful to an organization's stakeholders - who include all the participants in the system: management, employees, consumers and share holders (if any), affected communities, and other systems that might be collaborating with the organization. The first feature is that together we represent a diverse wealth of life experiences, that we're comfortable sharing our ideas with each other, and believe that working together may help us find new ways of solving old problems. That means listening to each contributor's observations as well as offering our own, by the way.

Type casting is an important concept here, particularly in assigning responsibilities in the work force. Since we vary a lot in our skills and interests, each of us will perform best if we do what comes naturally and what we are trained to do. Promotion is not a blessing when it moves us from a job we love and do well to one which we hate, and for which we have no talent. You've probably seen examples of such mismatches in your own work world.

A familiar example of team management in public Institutions involves the United States Constitution and our national government. Our leaders, the president and vice president, are elected by U.S. citizens and/or by " the people's representatives" (the electoral college). The president then appoints a cabinet of department directors to help run the government. The organization(s) run by each department head carry out the responsibilities and duties in that department's charge.

In addition, we have representatives and senators, also elected by the people. They serve in the Congress. They create and modify our laws and appropriate the funds to run the government. The president then signs or vetoes these laws and appropriations, and conducts the business of the country within their limits. The Congress can override the president's veto if two-thirds of the members vote to do so. The president serves for no longer than two terms of four years. Representatives must be elected or re-elected every two years, and senators run every six years.

To provide another check and balance for decisions made by either the president or the Congress, nine judges (who are appointed for life) serve on the Supreme Court and rule on the constitutionality of any decisions or laws which are challenged as contrary to the mandates of our Constitution. When a vacancy occurs on the Supreme Court, the president, with advice and consent of the Senate, appoints a judge from a lower court to fill the vacancy.

*   *   *   *   *

Since both the Leadership Team (the president and the vice president) and the Congress are chosen by the citizens of our country to represent them, how they interpret that responsibility is crucial to the way they govern. Some who are elected assume that they have been chosen to speak for the people, using their own judgment of what is in the best interests of the people. Others feel that they should listen carefully to what the voters say they want - and work to achieve those preferences.

Clearly, it is important that we understand this difference. Do we want to "be led" by those we elect, or do we want them to "reflect our own thinking" as they make and enforce our laws and appropriate and spend our taxes. We should vote accordingly.

Chapter 6

Putting It All Together

So where do we go from here? What does all this mean to you?

Where you are right now is your starting point for the rest of your life. All of your accumulated experiences have been stored in that "little black box" located in your brain. This is a continuing process for each of us for as long as we live, and you're better at who <u>you</u> are than anyone else.

What about that "black box?" Each of us has a characteristic which I like to call <u>virtuosity</u>. I first became aware of it when I was trying to learn how to play the piano. First, of course, I had to master techniques to finger the scales. Then I began playing simple pieces, and since I had pretty good musical sense, I did pretty well. It was when I tried more complicated works that I ran into trouble. I couldn't seem to think fast enough to play the runs.

My piano teacher pointed out to me that once I'd learned all the technical tricks so they came easily, I needed to stop trying to control every note and to let my brain and my reflexes guide my performance. Each of our brains has two parts, conscious, and unconscious. We experience most of our learning with the conscious part; our unconscious gray matter links each bit of learning to other experiences which are already stored in our brains, and this adds color and meaning to it all.

This important human ability allows us to combine skills, talents, and experiences stored in each of our own "black boxes" with the input that we continually acquire through experience and practice. It is probably best demonstrated by "virtuoso" soloists both in music and in sports. Time after time, they offer performances unmatched by most of us. What comes out is an intuitive combination of the conscious and the unconscious which is greater than either could produce alone.

I believe that this process, which requires us to have faith that it will happen, is present and can be tapped in all of us to some degree. It is also a component of serendipitous outputs which seem to come out of nowhere. But its manifestation is interfered with by too much conscious attention to how we're rendering our own performance. This is why you can carry a cup of coffee across a room without spilling it if you look ahead and don't watch the cup. Your body has long since learned how to balance things that you carry. If you try to consciously control the action, you block access to what your body already knows how to do.

*   *   *   *   *

Have you ever noticed that it often takes much longer than you planned to complete what you started out to do? Living is sometimes defined as what we do while we're making plans for our future. When I look back on my own dreams as a child, I find that I've taken a very different path than I dreamed about. During my journey, I kept having new experiences and learning new things while the world around me changed. And, of course, I adjusted to those changes.

Moreover, it's on purpose that I've seldom labeled the phenomena that I've described so far as "good" or "bad," The main indicators of success in the evolutionary processes of living systems are "survival" and "growth" of one kind or another, just as the main signs of failure are "increasing entropy" and "eventual death." This is true for all levels of living systems from cells to supranational systems. But Nature is in no hurry for either success or failure to happen. We all have built-in mechanisms for getting back into harmonic balance whenever we deviate from a steady state position.

The almost unlimited potential of becoming a human being plays out differently for each of us as we mature and find our own special route. But it is useful for us to realize that our bodies are our primary instruments for performing our souls' missions. Each of us will find more meaning in our existence if we try to live the particular life that we feel we were born to live. It's also imperative that we take the best possible care of our bodies, so they are there for us when we need them.

The relationship between biological and social evolution is tricky. Homo sapiens is, indeed, the only surviving species with a brain that not only permits but also often requires us to choose among alternative possibilities when we make decisions about our behavior. For other species, the way they behave is largely wired into their biochemical systems, leading to much less variability in behavior patterns within the species. The human brain is also biologically based, so many common characteristics also underlie and provide limitations in our behavior.

When we perceive a new threat, we still experience a "fight or flight" reaction, even though we've learned that neither fight nor flight may be appropriate in our modern world. But we can call on our socially learned choices to counteract the threat with tactics which will work in our evolving civilization. Nonetheless, wherever we have landed throughout the world, across races, generations, and geographic locations, we still seek out mates to procreate and cluster into nuclear families to protect and raise our children, much as many other species do.

As we study ancient civilizations from all over the world, it's striking how similarly they are organized even though they arose in different centuries and markedly different areas of that world. Early civilizations, for instance, with little scientific evidence to go by, believed that when their dear ones died, they would quite literally need preservation of their bodies, food, clothes and tools to help them move physically into the "next world." Even though they lived in widely separated times and continents, ancient Egyptian and Mayan cultures both developed pyramids for burial quarters to achieve this, as well as extensive hieroglyphics to record their histories.

Actually, there are lots of models in evolving biogenic communities which we can learn from as we try to assure that our ability to make choices, with all of our potential for producing change, moves us toward harmony with each other rather than toward mutual destruction. Coral reefs, for instance, have achieved a long-standing balance between predators and prey where hundreds of marine species coexist in perpetual self-sustaining communities.

Until humans came along and began dominating (and often destroying) what Nature has sustained for ages, these reefs and their communities survived nicely. Our propensity for remodeling the environment to favor our "creature comforts" is rapidly destroying these biologically evolved wonders. And since their behavior patterns are tightly wired into each species, and ours are not, we can usually call the shots. Sadly, we seem to be better at using our brains to destroy natural phenomena in this world that we all inhabit than we are at creating ways to preserve them.

Before I close this story about our planet's never-ending evolutionary processes, I need to emphasize an accelerating trend in the social evolution of the human species. As we learn about, develop, and apply knowledge acquired primarily through scientific exploration, we're discovering new ways to use both non-living systems and lower forms of living systems to enhance human survival and growth.

For example, our expertise in electronics already allows anyone with a modern computer to communicate easily with other humans all over the world, regardless of language differences. NASA is already sending robots to Mars, our nearest neighbor. Those technological marvels will transmit details back to us about its characteristics to use in our quest for mastery over space.

At the same time, medical specialists have begun to send signals to robots that help other doctors operate on people, though in some cases the specialists may be hundreds of miles away from the locus of the operation. Our rapid growth in understanding how pharmaceutical agents act in our bodies gives promise of our potential to live longer, healthier lives.

Charting of the human genome has opened up new and exciting possibilities for medical research to cure previously incurable diseases. New knowledge about stem cells may allow us to replace injured tissue - even in our brains - while robotic appliances can often substitute, where necessary, for other essential organs in our bodies. Thus, there appears to be no end to our potential to overcome all obstacles to our successful thriving as a species.

But you may have already guessed that there's a "however" lurking in the background here. Again I refer you to our amazing brains, and our ability to make choices. The choices we make, and the way we choose to make them, will help determine whether Homo sapiens prospers or flounders. Our growth of knowledge about "how to do things" is flourishing, but are we far enough along in our social evolution to have the wisdom we need to accompany the knowledge? Can our value systems and our sense of "oneness" as a species survive the temptations that we are feeling? Will we let selfishness and desire for privilege and control of those who get in our way triumph over enlightened self-interest, collaboration, and mutual trust and respect among all the stakeholders?

Our ongoing struggle in Iraq provides an excellent example of the down side of our blossoming mastery over military technology. Over the years, we have been able to get further and further away from the damage we inflict on both "the enemy" and our own forces during war. Thus it gets easier to develop and apply ever more destructive weapons without anyone except those directly on the battlefield having to get anywhere near the blood, gore, and tragedy befalling those in the way - guilty or innocent.

We get caught up in the glories of patriotic struggle, particularly after a long period without a declared war (which dulls our memories of the last one). It's not until the body bags and the still living but badly mutilated veterans start coming home that we have any sense of the tragedies we have wrought. Though we can't undo what we've already done, in previous campaigns we've been able to step back and start over, vowing that this time we've learned from our mistakes.

We've certainly demonstrated that we can make war. We're good at coming together to do the bidding of hierarchical leaders. We've had a lot of practice at this. But can we learn how to make peace before we destroy ourselves altogether? Can we make team management really work at a global level? That's the major choice involved in this example.

As we watch forest fires, flooded rivers, and hurricane-strength winds destroy communities across our land, we can hope that we are smart enough to reverse these trends which are magnified by our pursuit of immediate gratification. As the richest and most powerful nation on earth, who better than we to show how to establish homeostatic balances in our environmental practices? But that means avoiding excesses and privileged extravagance in order to restore biogenic harmony

76

and to maintain steady states all over the earth. Are we wise enough to do this while we still have a choice?

*   *   *   *   *

Currently, we're destroying those balances as we maintain a growing multitude of corporate assembly lines of cows to produce milk. Large farms are converted to mass breeding and processing factories to overload our markets with pork. Large corporations are making huge profits, which, for them, apparently justify the resultant pollution of our farmlands and our rivers with the wastes of the animals that they electronically herd and mass produce. Will we take action to outlaw such abuses before we contaminate our land beyond recovery, and guarantee the accompanying extinction of the farm families that used to maintain a harmonious balance between need and production?

Make no mistake: there is a rhythm and harmony in living. Nature's laws are always there - however hard we try to ignore them. When we pay attention to them, our daily decisions lead to better outcomes for us. Then Nature's laws work with us instead of against us. We sometimes don't notice this because the time spans of both biological and social evolution stretch out on both sides of our own life spans.

There are, however, general principles for successful evolutionary growth for living systems, both biogenic and sociogenic, which have not changed over time and which still operate. We can try to ignore them or get around them, but we can't change them. Successful, meaningful living is more likely for us if we recognize their existence and build our lives in harmony with them.

So, how do we move toward improving our harmony with the evolving rhythms of social evolution? Nature's laws are economical and usually have widespread applications. Across the ages of evolutionary development from the beginning of time, some basic rules have applied:

• <u>Introduce change and try it out over time.</u> What works will survive. What doesn't will deteriorate and die.

• <u>Learn from failure, and build on success.</u> As your foundation for change, use the already existing assets in the situation.

• <u>Be aware that time always moves ahead</u>. We can never change what has already happened. Learn and move on.

As living systems developed on our planet Earth, a new rule addressed their ever more complex levels of organization.

• <u>Look for similarities across evolving levels</u>. Strategies which have worked in simpler systems may suggest principles which will help us to design workable solutions for more complex systems.

The emergence of the human species and our capability to choose the direction and extent of our social evolution has created a potential to develop both enhanced survival and growth and increased risk of self-destruction. It's in choosing between these alternatives that we have the most to gain - or lose.

*   *   *   *   *

As a general rule, Nature's way begins simply, trying out many alternative types of responses to challenge. Nature also often uses the same solutions to address more than one issue. These examples build as they move from the simplest to more and more complex versions, each of which puts the developing system in a little better shape to deal with the issue.

This suggests that in our quest to solve problems or design new strategies, we need to start with local, site-specific inputs from those with the most experience in trying to overcome the challenge. Once they have developed a model, which works for them, other groups who might want to use it should try it out. They will need to make whatever modifications are necessary to make it a better fit for them, but most of the time they shouldn't need to start from scratch.

As our social organizations branch out and grow in complexity, they should seek input from many varied sources of information and perspective related to the issue or challenge being addressed. The objective is to create designs and schemes where all those who will be affected by the outcome have opportunities for input, allowing them some degree of satisfaction with the result. Such strategies move us toward harmony rather than discord in our relationships with each other.

Social evolution depends on our capability to try out many varieties of creative and flexible behavior available to human beings. We continuously make choices in the way we design and modify our organizational living systems. As we construct our laws and regulations, they will be most effective when they reflect group consensus about which of the numerous possible ways of doing things the group has chosen to follow.

When our judgment about what's needed contradicts existing laws, the laws need to be changed by unleashing the potential of our collective brains and thinking together to provide better solutions. An inflexible rule which assumes that "one size fits all who are affected by it" is never better than one which takes into account important differences among us which make the rule less appropriate to follow.

* * * * *

To give you some sense of how powerful this approach can be, I'd like to cite two international examples that have functioned throughout the world for several decades and continue today to fill crying needs in communities all over the world.

The first, and perhaps the most familiar to most of us is Habitat for Humanity International. A church-based organization with headquarters in Americus, Georgia, they partner with volunteers all over the world, from all walks of life, to build and renovate houses with and for families in need. These families then own decent homes in decent communities with a chance to raise their children as part of those communities.

The second organization, also church-based and volunteer activated, is Heifer International. Their headquarters are in Little Rock, Arkansas, and their mission is to help people around the world fight hunger and become self-reliant. Their name grew out of their first shipment of dairy animals to Puerto Rico in 1944. The kinds of living creatures they supply depends on where the families in need are located. In various locations, depending on the local environment, they have provided earthworms to help improve the soil for farming, bees for honey and to aid pollination, camels for desert transportation, and alpacas and llamas for wool and packing power in the high Andes.

From the beginning, in each of its projects, Heifer has required people who receive help to pass on to others in need a few offspring from the animals they were given by Heifer, as well as the training which they have received in animal husbandry. This spreads the benefits far beyond the original recipients to many millions of people.

*   *   *   *   *

I indicated early in this book that I have found many tried and true quotations from history especially valuable in helping me to make good choices during my own long and eventful life. I'd like to share a few of my favorites with you.

The first reflects the foundation for mutual trust which is so necessary for people to think productively together: "This above all, to your own self be true, and it shall follow as the day the night. You cannot then be false to anyone."

The second is crucial for helping us work together to build one harmonious world: "And you shall know the truth, and the truth shall make you free."

The third, which is so valuable to folks who are recovering from addictions, contains important advice for all of us. "God grant me the serenity to accept the things I cannot change, the courage to change the things I can, and the wisdom to know the difference."

Afterword
You're On Your Own

Some of you may want to delve deeper into one or another of the ideas - or ramifications of those ideas - which this book suggests.

• The model for living systems which allowed me to link the numerous varied phenomena which we have explored together is explained in great detail in: <u>Miller, James Grier: Living Systems, New York, McGraw-Hill, Inc. 1978.</u> It contains 1054 pages of readable and well-illustrated narrative followed by 52 pages of biographical and subject indices which should help you to locate whatever specific topics you want to read about.

• A comprehensive description of the theory of evolution - from the voyage of <u>Charles Darwin</u> which resulted in his book, <u>The Origin of Species</u>, through history to twenty-first century science exists in: <u>Zimmer, Carl: Evolution - The Triumph of an Idea. New York, Harper Collins 2001. (A companion volume to the PBS video series)</u>. It contains 344 pages of readable and well-illustrated narrative followed by a 20-page listing of further readings related to subjects covered in the book.

• Another book worth exploring is <u>The Sacred Balance, A Visual Celebration of Our Place in Nature by David Suzuki and Amanda McConnell, Greystone Books, Vancouver, Toronto & New York, 2003</u>. This book offers a photographic exploration of the web of life that unites all living things.

• Should you care to investigate their activities further, the address of Habitat for Humanity International is P.O. Box 1729, Americus, GA 31709-9948, and the address of Heifer International is 1015 Louisiana Street, Little Rock, AR 72202/ USA.